Lots of love

Today and Beyond

In Celebration of:

_____

_____

Date: _____

Guests

Name

Advice & Wishes

Guests

Name

Advice & Wishes

Guests

Name

Advice & Wishes

Guests

Name

Advice & Wishes

Guests

Name

Advice & Wishes

Guests

Name

Advice & Wishes

Guests

Name

Advice & Wishes

Guests

Name

Advice & Wishes

Guests

Name

Advice & Wishes

Guests

Name

Advice & Wishes

Guests

Name

Advice & Wishes

Guests

Name

Advice & Wishes

Guests

Name

Advice & Wishes

Guests

Name

Advice & Wishes

Guests

Name

Advice & Wishes

Guests

Name

Advice & Wishes

Guests

Name

Advice & Wishes

Guests

Name

Advice & Wishes

Guests

Name

Advice & Wishes

Guests

Name

Advice & Wishes

Guests

Name

Advice & Wishes

Guests

Name

Advice & Wishes

Guests

Name

Advice & Wishes

Guests

Name

Advice & Wishes

Guests

Name

Advice & Wishes

Guests

Name

Advice & Wishes

Guests

Name

Advice & Wishes

Guests

Name

Advice & Wishes

Guests

Name

Advice & Wishes

Guests

Name

Advice & Wishes

Guests

Name

Advice & Wishes

Guests

Name

Advice & Wishes

Guests

Name

Advice & Wishes

Guests

Name

Advice & Wishes

Guests

Name

Advice & Wishes

Guests

Name

Advice & Wishes

Guests

Name

Advice & Wishes

Guests

Name

Advice & Wishes

Guests

Name

Advice & Wishes

Guests

Name

Advice & Wishes

Guests

Name

Advice & Wishes

Guests

Name

Advice & Wishes

Guests

Name

Advice & Wishes

Guests

Name

Advice & Wishes

Guests

Name

Advice & Wishes

Guests

Name

Advice & Wishes

Guests

Name

Advice & Wishes

Guests

Name

Advice & Wishes

Guests

Name

Advice & Wishes

Guests

Name

Advice & Wishes

Guests

Name

Advice & Wishes

Guests

Name

Advice & Wishes

Guests

Name

Advice & Wishes

Guests

Name

Advice & Wishes

Guests

Name

Advice & Wishes

Guests

Name

Advice & Wishes

Guests

Name

Advice & Wishes

Guests

Name

Advice & Wishes

Guests

Name

Advice & Wishes

Guests

Name

Advice & Wishes

Guests

Name

Advice & Wishes

Guests

Name

Advice & Wishes

Guests

Name

Advice & Wishes

Guests

Name

Advice & Wishes

Guests

Name

Advice & Wishes

Guests

Name

Advice & Wishes

Guests

Name

Advice & Wishes

Guests

Name

Advice & Wishes

Guests

Name

Advice & Wishes

Guests

Name

Advice & Wishes

Guests

Name

Advice & Wishes

Guests

Name

Advice & Wishes

Guests

Name

Advice & Wishes

Guests

Name

Advice & Wishes

Guests

Name

Advice & Wishes

Guests

Name

Advice & Wishes

Guests

Name

Advice & Wishes

Guests

Name

Advice & Wishes

Guests

Name

Advice & Wishes

Guests

Name

Advice & Wishes

Guests

Name

Advice & Wishes

Guests

Name

Advice & Wishes

Guests

Name

Advice & Wishes

Guests

Name

Advice & Wishes

Guests

Name

Advice & Wishes

Guests

Name

Advice & Wishes

Guests

Name

Advice & Wishes

Guests

Name

Advice & Wishes

Guests

Name

Advice & Wishes

Guests

Name

Advice & Wishes

Guests

Name

Advice & Wishes

Guests

Name

Advice & Wishes

Guests

Name

Advice & Wishes

Guests

Name

Advice & Wishes

Guests

Name

Advice & Wishes

Guests

Name

Advice & Wishes

Guests

Name

Advice & Wishes

Guests

Name

Advice & Wishes

Guests

Name

Advice & Wishes

Guests

Name

Advice & Wishes

Guests

Name

Advice & Wishes

Guests

Name

Advice & Wishes

Guests

Name

Advice & Wishes

Guests

Name

Advice & Wishes

Guests

Name

Advice & Wishes

Guests

Name

Advice & Wishes

Guests

Name

Advice & Wishes

Guests

Name

Advice & Wishes

Guests

Name

Advice & Wishes

Guests

Name

Advice & Wishes

Guests

Name

Advice & Wishes

Guests

Name

Advice & Wishes

Guests

Name

Advice & Wishes

Guests

Name

Advice & Wishes

Guests

Name

Advice & Wishes

Guests

Name

Advice & Wishes

Guests

Name

Advice & Wishes

Guests

Name

Advice & Wishes

Made in the USA
Middletown, DE
23 June 2022

67646346R00071